Prayers for HEALING and DELIVERANCE
Vol. 1

A spiritual prescription for the release of divine health, peace and restoration

BETTY JAMISON

Copyright © 2019 Betty Jamison
ISBN 978-1-7323126-4-7

All Rights Reserved.

No part of this book may be reproduced or transmitted in any form or by any means, electronically or mechanically, including photocopying, recording or by an information storage and retrieval system without permission in writing from the author or publisher of this book.

Scripture taken from the New King James Version®. Copyright © 1982 by Thomas Nelson. Used by permission. All rights reserved.

Disclaimer:
We believe God can bring healing and deliverance through spiritual wisdom, medical wisdom and a positive lifestyle change on your part. When using this prayer resource, in no way, do we advocate or encourage you to refrain from medical treatment as prescribed to you by the medical community. Use this resource by faith, in conjunction with your prescribed medical treatment and any necessary lifestyle changes that will benefit your overall health. When purchasing or using this resource, you agree you release the author, publisher, and any person or entity associated with this resource, from any liability or perceived negligence.

Interior & Cover Layout and Design:
Tarsha L. Campbell

Published by:
DOMINIONHOUSE
Publishing & Design, LLC
P.O. Box 681938 | Orlando, Florida 32868 | 407.703.4800
www.mydominionhouse.com

———————— Dedication ————————

I would like to dedicate this book to everyone who is experiencing a health and deliverance battle. May the prayers within these pages infuse you with new life and new hope.

"Then your light shall break forth like the morning, your healing shall spring forth speedily, And your righteousness shall go before you; The glory of the Lord shall be your rear guard."
(Isaiah 58:8)

Acknowledgment

First, I want to acknowledge my mother, Deaconess Everlina Dixon for your legacy of prayer, and for your example in prayer and intercession. Thank you for being a constant support of love, and encouragement.

I gratefully acknowledge my family, my children, grandchildren, and great grandchildren. You have truly motivated, challenged, stimulated, and inspired me to pray. Thank you!!!

Special thanks to Prophet George Carter, Jr. for saying, "yes" to accompanying me for the CD for this project. Bless you man of God.

Special thanks to Melissa Rentz, my personal intercessor. Thank you for covering me everyday.

I wish to acknowledge my Pastors, Apostle Willie and Prophetess Linda King for the impact you have made in my life. Thank you for covering me.

I want to acknowledge all the prayer warriors, intercessors, and watchmen of the Watchmen on the Wall Prayer Network: Sherrie Singleton, Edwina Ross, Patricia Banks, Delois Holland, Leticia Lamar, Shima Clark, Anita Neal Okaro, Apostle Dena Elmore, Dr. Leslie Miller, Dr. Myrtle Newbold, Dr. Laronda Brown, Deborah Wright and all I couldn't name. I appreciate you.

Lastly, I wish to acknowledge Prophetess Tarsha and Dwayne Campbell. You have lifted up my arms and aided me in so many endeavors. You have been a blessing in many times of need. I am grateful and thankful for you being in my life. To Tarsha, thank you for your expertise, and for being my coach, my encourager, also for your patience and belief in this assignment. I couldn't have done it without you. Thank you!!!

> *But He was wounded for our transgressions,*
> *He was bruised for our iniquities;*
> *The chastisement for our peace was upon Him,*
> *And by His stripes we are healed."*
> *(Isaiah 53:5)*

Table of Contents

Foreword 9

Healing Prayer for Cancer 17

Healing Prayer for the Spirit of Depression 21

Healing Prayer for Depression in Children 25

Healing Prayer for Anxiety 29

Healing Prayer for Osteoarthritis 32

Healing Prayer for Alzheimer's Disease 35

Healing Prayer for Rheumatoid Arthritis 38

Healing Prayer for Sickle Cell Anemia 41

Healing Prayer for Emotional Healing 43

Healing Prayer for Asthma 45

Healing Prayer for Strokes 47

Healing Prayer for Lupus 50

Healing Prayer for ADHD 53

Prayer Request Journal 57

Praise Reports 62

More Resources to Help 63

About the Author 64

Prayer Support 66

"Beloved, I pray that you may prosper in all things and be in health, just as your soul prospers."
(3 John 2)

FOREWORD

Who Himself bore our sins in His own body on the tree, that we, having died to sins, might live for righteousness—by whose stripes you were healed.
1 Peter 2:24

It is God's will that you be healed. Yes, you read that right. It is God's will and desire that you live a life free from sickness, disease, and affliction.

There are a plethora of scriptures that indicate healing to be a covenant promise between Our Father God and His children.

One such scripture that comes to mind is Psalm 107:20:

> He sent his word, and healed them, and delivered them from their destructions.

Psalm 103:2-5 is another convincing indicator that Father God desires for you to walk in divine healing and deliverance, and through this, you are revitalized with divine strength.

> Bless the Lord, O my soul, and forget not all His benefits: Who forgives all your iniquities, Who heals all your diseases, Who redeems your life from destruction, Who crowns you with lovingkindness and Who satisfies your mouth with good things, so that your youth is renewed like the eagle's.

By his loving hand and tender mercies, God has extended the promise to taste of His healing grace and transformative power of deliverance.

When Psalm 107:20 states, "He sent his word, and healed them, and delivered them from their destructions," I don't believe it only refers to the written word of God we read in the Bible. I believe it also alludes to Christ the Messiah coming in bodily form as the *Word* of life to redeem us from sin, as well as from the ailments of our spirit, soul, and body. Let's look at John 1:1-2, 14 (NKJV):

Foreword

> In the beginning was the Word, and the Word was with God, and the Word was God. He was in the beginning with God.
>
> And the Word became flesh and dwelt among us, and we beheld His glory, the glory as of the only begotten of the Father, full of grace and truth.

I believe these verses are key. Christ is the *Word* sent to heal and deliver us from our destructions. The finished work of Christ didn't just come to save your soul from sin, but it also provided provision for healing and deliverance too.

In Romans 10:8-10, we catch another glimpse of God's saving and healing power through His Son Jesus Christ. It reads:

> But what does it say? "The word is near you, in your mouth and in your heart" (that is, the word of faith which we preach): that if you confess with your mouth the Lord Jesus and believe in your heart that God has raised Him from the dead, you will be saved.

> For with the heart one believes unto righteousness, and with the mouth confession is made unto salvation.

This is so powerful! As I did a more in depth study of the words "saved" and "salvation" as used in this scripture passage, I found the meaning of these two words as conveyed in the original language this text was written in. These meanings pointed to a more comprehensive extent of Christ's saving power.

The word "saved" in Greek is "sōzō". This word means to save a suffering one (from perishing), i.e. one suffering from disease, to make well, heal, restore to health. It also means to deliver and protect.

The word "salvation" in Greek is "sōtēria". This word means to rescue or bring to safety (physically or morally): to provide deliverance, health, and to save.

Glory! Through the finished work of Christ (who was the bodily manifestation of the *Word* sent to deliver us), we can have access to the divine health, healing, and deliverance provided by the Father.

Foreword

I don't know about you, but that pushes my faith to a whole new level! I'm inclined to believe God wants more than to save me from my sins. But He wants me to be healed and delivered too.

With that said, I want to invite you to grab hold to the *Word* of healing and deliverance presented in this book through these life-altering prayers of faith. I personally know the mighty vessel of honor, Pastor Betty Jamison, who has meticulously researched the health conditions addressed in this book and written these powerful prayers to stand against these debilitating conditions. She has also taken it a step further and recorded a companion CD and digital downloads these prayers so she can walk along side you to declare your freedom from these devastating ailments.

Not only can I attest to her due diligence to produce a prayer resource that will get results, but as her daughter, I am also aware of the personal journey she has taken to receive her own divine intervention for healing and deliverance. It was through the power of the *Word*, in praying and confessing it, that Pastor Jamison victoriously overcame a battle with cancer over 40 years ago, and she has never had a reoccurrence of this infirmity in her body. During her faithful walk with God, she has not only gained victory for herself, but for many others by "prescribing" life-saving prayers infused with the Word of God.

As a result of her victories, we would like to encourage you to use this book and the companion CD or digital downloads of the prayers as "spiritual prescriptions" for healing and deliverance. You are advised to use it alongside any treatment the health community has instructed you to follow. Just as you are instructed to take a medication prescription at or during a specific time, you are encouraged to treat the prayers that address your needs or the needs of your loved ones as "spiritual prescriptions". You can also use the prayers daily as a "spiritual supplement" similar to how one may take daily vitamins and mineral supplements. By faith in God's power to heal and the finished work of Christ, read the prayers out loud with the CD or digital download and expect divine results.

Remember that it is God's will that you experience His healing and delivering power. I come in agreement with you that divine health, deliverance, and peace will be your portion as you use this resource. May you experience the lovingkindness and tender mercies of the Father to heal and deliver you, in Jesus' matchless name. Amen.

Tarsha Campbell
Minister, Author, Certified Coach,
and Woman of Faith
www.TarshaCampbellEmpowers.com

> *Bless the Lord, O my soul,*
> *And forget not all His benefits:*
> *Who forgives all your iniquities,*
> *Who heals all your diseases."*
> *(Psalms 103:2-3)*

HEALING PRAYER FOR CANCER

Sovereign God, in the mighty name of Jesus, I exalt and honor you for being the great I AM in our life. I thank you for being the Lord of Lords, and the King of Kings. You are the Lamb that was slain from the foundation of the world and worthy to be praised. I acknowledge you and say thank you for being my redeemer, my healer, my deliverer, my burden-bearer, and the lifter up of my head.

You told me in first Peter, the fifth chapter and the seventh verse, to cast my cares upon you because you care for me. I plead the blood of Jesus over my mind. It is written in St. John the tenth chapter and the tenth verse that the enemy comes to steal, kill, and to destroy, but Jesus came that I might have life and have it more abundantly. I declare that God has not given me a spirit of fear, but of love, power, and a sound mind. In Jesus' name, I speak peace to my mind. The word of God says in Psalm one hundred and eighteen verse seventeen, that I shall live and not die and declare the works of the Lord. Lord you said in St. John the six chapter and the sixty-third verse that your word is spirit and it is life. I speak life to myself today.

Lord, I thank you for sending your word and for healing me from destruction according to Psalm one hundred and seven and verse twenty. I decree and declare into the universe that you are my healer and deliverer. I decree and declare, my body is the temple of the Holy Ghost and no unclean thing shall dwell in it.

Lord, you said in Matthew the fifteen chapter and the thirteenth verse, that every plant that you have not planted, shall be rooted up! According to your word, I speak to every abnormal cell, tumors and growths that invade and spread throughout the body [the brain, the breast, prostate, ovaries, cervix, liver, kidneys, lungs, pancreas, and stomach and the other areas that cancer attacks me. You are trespassing. In Jesus' name, I command you to dry up from the root and die. Through the power of the shed blood of Jesus, the Word, the Holy Spirit, and the name of Jesus, your assignment is canceled.

Body, in Jesus' name, I apply the blood against abnormal bleeding, lumps, growths, tumors, prolonged coughs, and unexplained weight loss. I call forth divine healing and deliverance now. I command my body to line up with the word of God and be healed.

For life and death are in the power of the tongue. You said we could choose life and live, or death and die. You said we could have what we say. I choose life in Jesus' name. You said all things are possible to them that believe. Lord, I believe you can restore me to complete health. I touch and agree with the Holy Spirit by faith through the power of the spoken word, for the anointing to destroy every yoke and the gift of healing to manifest in Jesus' name. I curse cancer and every symptom to the root. In Jesus' name, I command every cancer cell to die. Ministering angels, move supernaturally throughout the universe bringing healing, deliverance and curing me and all who are afflicted by this deadly infirmity. Thank you for hearing my prayer, and for setting me and the captive free. Amen, amen.

HEALING PRAYER FOR THE SPIRIT OF DEPRESSION

Father God, I thank you for this day, because this is the day that you have made. I shall rejoice and be glad in it. I thank you for your grace and for your mercies, because your mercies are brand new every day. If it had not been for your mercies I would have been consumed. You are the author and finisher of my faith, and for this I tell you thank you. You are the Lamb of God, the wonderful counselor, the prince of peace, my healer, and deliverer, for this I tell you thank you. You are awesome and so worthy to be praised. To you be the glory for the things you have done.

As I come into your presence, I acknowledge you as my redeemer. I ask you to forgive me for my sins, transgressions, and blot out my iniquities and remember them no more. Create in me a clean heart and renew a right spirit within me. You said in Psalms 66:18, if I regard iniquity in my heart, you will not hear me. Lord, I need you to hear me as I stand in prayer against depression.

According to your word in James the fifth chapter and verses fourteen and fifteen, you said, "If there is any sick among us, we are to call for the elders of the church, and they are to pray over the sick, anointing them with oil in the name of Jesus. And the prayer of faith shall save the sick. And the Lord shall raise him up: and if they have committed sins, they shall be forgiven."

Today Lord God, I lift up all forms of depression: bipolar depression, postpartum depression, and clinical depression. I expose the root causes and apply the ax of God's word in Jesus' name to hormonal imbalances, the negative side effects of medications and drugs (legal and illegal) such as: antidepressants, steroids, cardiac medications, chronic illness, thyroid deficiency, melancholy temperament, and inherited traits.

By faith, I repent and confess my sins asking for forgiveness of disobedience, bitterness, anger, fear of rejection, stress, grief, guilt, and negative self-talk. I offer my heart to you Lord for cleansing. You said in 1 John chapter one verses eight, and nine, "If we claim we are without sin, we deceive ourselves and the truth is not in us. You said if we confess our sins, you are faithful and just to forgive our sins and will purify us from all unrighteousness." For this cause Jesus was manifested that he might destroy the works of the devil.

By the authority of the word, the name of Jesus, and the Holy Spirit, I bind up any mood disorder impacting me, such as postpartum depression, bipolar depression, cycles of depression, mania, clinical depression, and major depression. I take authority over every symptom that involves the body, thoughts, and moods. In Jesus' name, I bind up spirits of sadness, loneliness, tearfulness, emptiness, hopelessness, angry outbursts, irritability, frustration, insomnia, sleeping to much, tiredness, fatigue, weight loss, cravings, anxiety, agitation, restlessness, worthlessness, self-blame of past failures, physical problems, recurrent thoughts of death, attempts of suicide or suicide.

I release the anointing of peace into the atmosphere right now. Angels on assignment, move in response to this prayer, breaking every yoke and canceling every assignment in Jesus' name. You said you would keep us in perfect peace when our mind is stayed on you. In Jesus' name, by faith, I plead the blood over my mind. I take authority over every mind-binding spirit. I command you to loose your hold. I call forth the miracle working power of the Lord Jesus Christ to set me free. Holy Spirit, help me to put on the garment of praise for the spirit of heaviness. Manifest yourself through this prayer as I apply your word. In Jesus' name, angels go now to bring forth healing, breakthrough, and deliverance.

I close this prayer with this question and answer from Psalm 42:5. Why art thou cast down, O my soul? And why art thou disquieted in me? By faith in the blood of Jesus, the word of God, the power of the Holy Spirit, and the name of Jesus I hope in God: for I shall yet praise him for the help of his countenance. You Lord God are my help. Amen.

HEALING PRAYER FOR DEPRESSION IN CHILDREN

Lord God, in Jesus' name, I acknowledge you as the great I am. There is nothing too hard for you. You are Jehovah-Rapha, our healer and Jehovah-Rophe, the great physician. I thank you for sending your word and healing us and for delivering us from destruction.

You said in Hebrews 4:16, to come boldly unto the throne of grace, that we may obtain mercy, and find help in time of need. I thank you for this opportunity to bring unto you, my child who struggles with the spirit of depression. As their intercessor, in Jesus' name, I plead the blood over them. I cancel the assignment of depression and expose every common sign and symptom that oppress them. I cast down sadness, irritability, clinginess, worry, ache, pains, insomnia, fears, excuses to keep them from going to school, and being overweight. I cast these cares upon you because you care for them.

In Jesus' name, I pray for your yoke destroying power of healing and deliverance to be manifested in their lives to heal them from all traumatic experiences, family conflicts, emotional abuse, verbal abuse, sibling rivalry, bullying, and inherited mental illness. As I lift them up to you, I release the peace of God to guard their heart and mind in Christ Jesus. Angels go now and cause healing to be released. I thank you that there is no distance in prayer.

As their intercessor, I lift up my child. I ask forgiveness for their sins. I pray for your grace and mercy for the depressed. In Jesus' name, I ask you to lift them out of the pit of despair and despondency. I decree and declare deliverance and breakthrough from thoughts of worthlessness, poor self-image, isolation, anger, behavior problems, drug use, abuse of alcohol, and self-harm.

I ask you to be a hiding place and shield against bullying. I bind up peer pressure, and gang affiliation. I bring before you Lord, hurts, pains, discouragement, rejections, frustrations, suicidal thoughts, self-mutilations, searching for love and approval in the wrong places, and learning disabilities. I lay my child at the foot of Jesus. I loose the anointing of the blood over their mind by faith. I stand on their behalf asking you to supernaturally come to the rescue. I pray asking you to send godly men and women to mentor them.

You said in your word, you have already made a way of escape for them. I claim that way through salvation. I speak into the universe that they are no longer victims, but they are victors through Christ Jesus, and they are more than conquerors in Jesus' name. I declare by faith, your healing and miracle working power to supernaturally go into the dark crevices of their heart and mind and change them into a mighty vessel of God. I ask all these things in your son Jesus' name, our redeemer. Make them whole in thee.

By faith, I ask you to remove every weight, and spirit of heaviness off them. I pray for the garment of praise. I thank you for your grace and mercy. I thank you for being touched with the feelings of their infirmities. I thank you that your word says no weapon formed against them will prosper.

Lord, there is nothing to hard for you. As I pray, I ask you to set them free. I stand on the promise that all things are possible to them that believe. Lord, I believe. Thank you for divine intervention. Holy Spirit, breathe on them and overshadow them with your grace and mercy I pray. Amen.

HEALING PRAYER FOR ANXIETY

Father, I come again to give you thanks and praise for all you have done and all that you are going to do for me. I thank you for looking beyond my faults and seeing my needs. I thank you for being a very present help in the time of trouble. I thank you for your loving-kindness and tender mercies. I bless your name for supplying my every need. Thank you for being an awesome and faithful God.

You told me in Philippians, the fourth chapter, the sixth through the eighth verse, not to fret or have anxiety about anything, but in every circumstance and in everything, by prayer and petition, with thanksgiving, continue to make my wants known unto you. And the peace of God which pass all understanding, shall keep my heart and mind through Christ Jesus. You told me, if there be any virtue, if there be any praise, to think on those things that are true, honest, just, pure, lovely, and of a good report. For this we tell you thank you.

Lord, I come lifting up my voice in praise and thanksgiving in advance to you for turning every situation around. I thank you for this opportunity to cast all my cares and worries on you.

Holy Spirit, I ask you to take control of every situation that troubles my heart and mind. In Jesus' name, I ask for release from every form of emotional bondage that brings anxiety, worry, frustration, stress, aggravation, and fear.

Lord God, you told me not to worry or fret about anything. Just like you provide for the lilies of the field and the birds of the air, how much more will you take care of me. You told me submit unto God, and then resist the devil and he would flee.

You said, whatsoever I bind on earth you will bind in heaven, and whatsoever I loose on earth you will loose in heaven. By the Holy Spirit's power, I loose the spirit of peace, and the anointing to destroy every yoke, and lift every heavy burden off of me. I speak to every situation that releases stress, tension, worry, nervousness, depression, difficulty concentrating, feelings of restlessness, fatigue, trouble sleeping, and frustration. I apply the blood of Jesus. I will not bow. I will not fret or be anxious. I declare God is in control. Anxiety your assignment is canceled. I am free through the blood, the name of Jesus, and the spoken word of God. Lord, you said you will watch over your word to perform it in my life, and your word will not return to you empty. Angels of deliverance, angels of healing, angels of peace, war on our behalf in Jesus' name. I declare God's peace floods my mind as I seek His face. Thank you Lord for coming to the rescue. Amen. Amen. And amen.

HEALING PRAYER FOR OSTEOARTHRITIS

To God be the glory for the things He has done. Thank you for your grace and mercies, for they are brand new every day. Thank you for your infinite wisdom and your divine knowledge and understanding. Thank you for your blood that was shed on the cross for the sins of the whole world. I acknowledge you as the Lord of Lords, and the King of Kings, the mighty God, the prayer answering God. The God that looks beyond my faults and sees my needs. A very present help in the time of trouble.

Father, in the name of Jesus, I thank you for the power of the tongue. According to Proverbs 18:21, "Death and life are in the power of the tongue, and those who love it will eat its fruit."

Body, in Jesus name, Christ has redeemed me from the curse of the law by being made a curse for me.

Through the power of redemption, I have been made whole, mind, body, and soul. I command my body to line up with the Word of God. Osteoarthritis, you have oppressed me long enough. I call forth the supernatural miracle working power of the Holy Spirit to re-create my joints and restore my marrow, and re-create the cartilage in my knees. In Jesus' name, I plead the blood against stiffness, inflammation, pain, infections and swellings in my body.

Spirit of infirmity, I decree and declare that your work has been aborted. Thank you Lord for the anointing that destroys every yoke. I speak to the spirit of osteoarthritis, I loose you from your assignment of pain, and stiffness in my hands, arms, feet, and fingers. No longer will I suffer from the loss of mobility, that hinders my ability to function. I speak restoration of my cartilage. Lord you said, whatsoever I ask the Father in the name of Jesus I could have what I say. Body, line up with the word of God. I ask you Lord God to strengthen the muscles around the joints, strengthen my immune system to fight inflammation, swelling, pain, stiffness, and repair damaged joints.

I confess, renounce and shut all portals such as hidden roots of bitterness, un-forgiveness, envy, strife, jealousy and inherited generational curses. In Jesus' name, I claim the promise of God to restore my health. I call my joints and marrow into divine health. Amen, and amen.

HEALING PRAYER
FOR ALZHEIMER'S DISEASE

Most Holy God, the creator of all mankind, our strong tower. I come boldly to the throne of grace seeking your mercy to help in this needy time.

I thank you for this opportunity to bring before you our elders, our mothers, our fathers, aunts, uncles, grandmothers, grandfathers and myself who are under attack by the infirmities of Alzheimer's Disease and dementia.

You said in John 10:10, the thief come not, but for to steal, to kill, and to destroy: But you have come that we might have life, and that we might have it more abundantly.

According to Matthew, the sixteenth chapter and the nineteenth verse, you promised, whatsoever I bind on earth shall be bound in heaven: and whatsoever I loose on earth shall be loosed in heaven. I take authority over Alzheimer's and dementia and cancel it's assignment and effects that robs individuals of their mental functions and progressively destroy their memory.

In Jesus' name, Holy Spirit overshadow this situation, release the ministering angels that are assigned to each individual caught in this snare and destroy the yokes and remove the burden.

You said in Jeremiah, the thirty-third chapter and the third verse, to call on you and you will answer and show us great and mighty things which we know not of. Here I am Lord. I'm calling on your name Jesus. For you said at the sound of the name Jesus that every knee must bow and every tongue confess that you are Lord.

You are Lord over Alzheimer's and dementia. For this cause you were revealed to destroy the works of the devil. In Jesus' name, I plead the blood against the spirit of Alzheimer's Disease and dementia. Lord, you said I could decree a thing and you would establish it. I decree total restoration to the cells that cause mental functions. In Jesus' name, I bind up spirits of confusion, forgetfulness, memory loss and generational curses that cause mental dysfunction. I bind up mind-binding spirits, mind controlling spirits, mind-altering spirits, mental pressure, and mental torment.

I loose the peace of God to rest upon them and restore total memory recall. I decree and declare that they have a sound mind.

Lord, move supernaturally through the blood line to purge it of this infirmity. Cover our families now with the blood of Jesus. Through this prayer, I set up boundaries in the realm of the spirit to protect us from backlash and retaliation. Through the power of the spoken word, I decree and declare that no weapon that is formed against them shall prosper, every lying spirit of confusion, forgetfulness, and memory loss is canceled. Lord, I loose the afflicted and myself from mind control, mental pain, mental pressure, and all evil influences that work against the mind. In Jesus' name, we declare God's grace, and mercy prevails. We call forth your miracle working power of healing and deliverance. Thank you Lord for coming to the rescue. Amen.

HEALING PRAYER
FOR RHEUMATOID ARTHRITIS

I will bless the Lord, oh my soul and all that is within me, I will bless your holy name. For you have done great things for me. I bless you for being omniscient; the all knowing God. I bless your name because you are omnipotent; the all powerful God. There is nothing to hard for you. You are omnipresent; the universal God. You are here, there, and every where at the same time. Thank you for being our healer, Jehovah-Rapha, and our great physician, Jehovah-Rophe. Thank you for being touched with the feelings of my infirmities, and for sending your word and healing me.

LORD God, in the mighty name of Jesus, your word says that we all have sinned and come short of your glory. But if we would confess our sins, you would forgive us of our sins and cleanse us from all unrighteousness.

Today LORD God, before I go any further in this prayer, I repent of all my sins, transgressions, and iniquities that I have done. LORD, forgive me and cleanse me from all unrighteousness. I don't want anything to hinder this prayer. You told me that I could come boldly to the throne of grace, so here I am LORD seeking your face for deliverance, and healing from these diabolical attacks of rheumatoid arthritis.

Through the power and anointing of the Holy Spirit, the word of God, and the name of Jesus, I bind and sever the main root of this autoimmune disease called rheumatoid arthritis. I cancel the assignment of the body's immune system that attacks the lining of the joint capsule to destroy the cartilage and bone within the joint. I thank you for this opportunity to touch and agree for deliverance and healing. In Jesus' name, using the power of agreement, and the keys of binding and loosing, I bind up inflammation, swelling, infection, stiffness, and joint pain. Rheumatoid arthritis, I destroy your impact on my body (hands, wrists, shoulders, knees, and feet) by applying the blood of Jesus to every area that is affected. In Jesus' name, I call on the ministering angels to manifest supernatural restoration of joints, and cartilage, and give the immune system the ability to fight infections, swelling and inflammation throughout the whole body now. I call the body healed. Amen, amen, and amen.

HEALING PRAYER FOR SICKLE CELL ANEMIA

Lord God, in the mighty name of Jesus, I thank you today that you are Jehovah – Rapha the God that heals, repairs, mend, cure, and make whole. I thank you for being our high priest that's touched with the feelings of our infirmities. As I come before you, I ask you to forgive me of my sins, transgressions, and iniquities, because you said in Psalm 66:18 that if I regard iniquity in my heart you will not hear me. Lord as my healer, I need you to hear me as it relates to this inherited blood disorder called sickle cell anemia. I repent of the sins of my forefathers all the way back to the fourth generation that opened up the door for this inherited weakness in the bloodline.

Lord, you said to put you in remembrance of the things you have promised. According to Isaiah the fifty-third chapter and the fifth verse, Jesus was wounded for our transgressions, he was bruised for our iniquities: the chastisement of our peace was upon him, and with his stripes we were healed.

I ask you in the mighty name of Jesus to make me whole, cure me of this blood disorder with all its weaknesses, deficiencies, pain, fatigue, and infections. Move supernaturally in my bloodstream and perform a spiritual blood transfusion. Body and immune system line up with the word of God in Jesus' name. Amen, amen, and amen.

HEALING PRAYER FOR EMOTIONAL HEALING

Thank you Lord for being touched with the feelings of my infirmities. Lord, I thank you and praise you for your mercies that endure forever. No good thing will you withhold from me. Thank you for the anointing that destroys every yoke.

Father, in the mighty name of Jesus, your word says to speak to the mountain and command the mountain to be cast into the sea and doubt not in my heart, but believe that those things which I say will come to pass, then I will have whatsoever I say.

Today, I speak to the emotional infirmities of rejection, abandonment, bitterness, a broken heart, hurt, sadness, depression, trauma, self-sabotage, low self-esteem, un-forgiveness and negative past memory recall. In the name of Jesus, I ask for forgiveness, healing, and deliverance in every area of my life. Lord Jesus, the Word of God declares that for this cause you were manifested to destroy the works of the devil and to set the captive free, to bind up the brokenhearted, and to undo every heavy burden. In Jesus' name, I call on the Holy Spirit to anoint me to destroy every yoke and deliver me from being oppressed by the enemy.

You said to cast my cares on you because you care for me. I bring the anxieties, the fears, the frustrations, the emotional pain of abuse, feelings of hopelessness, addictions, depression, discouragement, past hurts, and failures to you. I bind up the mind binding spirits, every mind altering spirit, and every mind controlling spirit sent out against me. I lay them upon you in Jesus' name. Lord God, by the authority of your word, and the name of Jesus, I plead the blood over my mind and I thank you for restoring my health, peace, joy, and healing all my wounds. Amen, amen, and amen.

HEALING PRAYER FOR ASTHMA

Father in the mighty name of Jesus, I give you praise and honor for this day because this is the day that you have made. We shall rejoice and be glad in it. I thank you for the victory over all the power of the enemy through your shed blood. I thank you and praise your holy name for releasing your miracle working power of wholeness in this prayer.

Spirit of the living God, in the mighty name of Jesus, our savior, you promised in Joel the second chapter and the thirty-second verse, that whosoever shall call on the name of the Lord shall be delivered. I thank you in advance for supernaturally moving to deliver my soul in peace from the battle of asthma.

Lord you said in your word, in Mark, the eleventh chapter and the twenty-third verse, that whosoever shall say unto this mountain (asthma) be thou removed, and be thou cast into the sea; and shall not doubt in his heart, but shall believe that those things which he said shall come to pass: he or she shall have whatsoever they say.

In Jesus' name, I speak to the inside walls of my lungs that you will not become inflamed or swollen, and to the membranes in the lining of my airways you will not, I repeat, you will not form and give off excess mucus.

In Jesus' name, through the power of the Holy Spirit, I bind up and cast out every spirit that causes asthma attacks. I speak to inflammation, swellings, and excess mucus. I arrest your work and render it null and void, and inoperable along with every sign and symptom of shortness of breath, tightness or pain in the chest, coughing, wheezing, trouble sleeping because of the shortness of breath, and respiratory infections such as flu, colds, and pneumonia. At your word Father, I decree and declare that none of the weapons that are formed to create asthma will prosper, and through the shed blood of Jesus, I'm released from the power of darkness. Amen, amen, and amen.

HEALING PRAYER FOR STROKES

Lord God, in the amazing name of Jesus, you said in your word in St. John the fourteenth chapter and the fourteenth verse, if I shall ask anything in your name, you would do it. As I come before your throne, I acknowledge you as my healer and my deliverer, you are the mighty God, you are the prayer answering God, you look beyond my faults and see my needs. For this, I bless your name.

Father, your word says the enemy comes to steal, to kill, and to destroy. But you have come that I might have life and have it more abundantly. In 1 John, the third chapter and the eighth verse, you said for this cause was Jesus manifested to destroy the works of the devil. Through the power of the spoken word, I cancel the assignment of stroke the silent killer. I take authority over interruptions or reduced blood supply to the brain that deprives my brain of oxygen and nutrients that causes the brain cells to die. Lord Jesus, you said whatsoever I bind on earth you will bind in heaven. And whatsoever I loose on earth you will loose in heaven.

I bind up blocked arteries, broken blood vessels, blood clots, high blood pressure, trauma, brain hemorrhages, vascular malformations, mini-strokes, tumors, heart attacks, and generational curses associated with this infirmity. I take authority over worry, anxiety, stress, frustration, mental and emotional pressure, fear and aggravation. I plead the blood of Jesus over my mind. I call forth the anointing of peace in the midst of confusion. I call forth the anointing of healing and deliverance in Jesus' name.

Holy Spirit, move now on every visible symptom, every temporary or permanent disability, complications such as paralysis, difficulty talking or swallowing, memory loss, depression, pain, numbness and lost of feelings in left arm. Ministering angels of healing, restore, strengthen, repair and make me whole again. In Jesus' name, I command my body to come into divine alignment with the word of God and function as God has designed it to function in Jesus' name.

According to your word in Psalms the one hundred-thirty-eighth chapter and verse seven, you said though we walk in the midst of trouble, you will revive us. You said you shall stretch forth your hand against the wrath of our enemies, and your right hand shall save us.

In Job twenty-two verse twenty-eight, your word says, we shall decree a thing, and it shall be established unto us. I decree and declare your word into the universe that you LORD God will restore my health. I ask you to heal me, O LORD, and I shall be healed: Save me, and I shall be saved: for you are my praise. I claim these precious promises coming from Jeremiah thirty and verse seventeen for myself in your son Jesus' name. You said, "For I will restore health unto thee, and I will heal thee of thy wounds", saith the LORD. Amen. Amen. And amen.

HEALING PRAYER FOR LUPUS

Father God, in the mighty name of Jesus, I thank you for your grace and I thank you for your mercy. For your mercies are brand new everyday. I bless your name because you are the author and finisher of my faith. You are my burden-bearer, my strong tower, my redeemer and my healer. For this I say thank you.

According to your word in Hebrews the fourth chapter and the sixteenth verse, I thank you for this opportunity to come boldly to the throne of grace so I may obtain your mercy and find grace to help in this time of need. For this is a needy time in my life as I am suffering from this auto-immune disease called lupus. I come in the mighty name of Jesus asking for your holy anointed oil of healing and deliverance to be manifested in my body. I give you praise, honor, and glory in advance for what you will do in my life.

Today Lord God, I come lifting up my body that's being affected by this chronic inflammatory disease called lupus. In Jesus' mighty name, I apply your blood against the spirit of inflammation that attacks the systems of the body, the joints, the skin, the kidneys, the blood cells, the brain, the heart, and the lungs.

According to your word in Matthew, the eighteenth chapter and the eighteenth verse, you said whatsoever I bind on earth you will bind in heaven and whatsoever I loose on earth you will loose in heaven. In Jesus' name, by the authority of your word, I come into agreement and bind up every symptom of fatigue, fever, joint pain, stiffness, swelling, shortness of breath, chest pains, dry eyes, headaches, confusion, infections, skin legions, rashes, and memory loss. By the authority of your word, I loose lupus from it's abnormal function in the immune system that attacks its own tissues and organs. In Jesus' name, I expose your plans and render you inoperable and ineffective against me.

Holy Spirit, I ask you to supernaturally overshadow the immune system and give it the ability to resist weaknesses and impart strength. In Jesus' name I command the immune system to function and fight this inflammation.

By faith, I declare that every yoke is destroyed and I'm healed, delivered and set free. Now God, I ask you to hasten to perform your word according to Jeremiah the first chapter and the twelfth verse. Supernatural God, who specializes in miracles, signs, and wonders, manifest yourself now in Jesus' mighty name. Amen, amen, and amen.

HEALING PRAYER
FOR ADHD
(Attention-deficient/hyperactivity disorder)

Father God, in the amazing name of Jesus, I thank you for your word. You said that your word will not return to you void, but it will accomplish what you send it out to do. I thank you for your mercies that we are not consumed, because your compassion fails not. Great is thy faithfulness, O Lord. Thank you for new mercies every morning.

LORD God, I bring before you loved ones and people I know affected by the chronic condition called attention-deficit / hyperactivity disorder. You told us to cast our cares upon you because you care for us. You said call on you and you will answer and show me great and mighty things which I know not of. So here I am Lord, standing in the need of your supernatural miracle working power that sets the captive free.

I'm asking you to move miraculously for every child or individual that is having a problem staying focused, those who have difficulty following through on instructions, those who are constantly on the go, those with learning disabilities, those with behavior problems, those who struggle with low self-esteem, and troubled relationships. I know that you specialize in things that are impossible to man, but are possible with you. As your agent in the earth, I pray against every lying spirit, every spirit of deception, every untruth. In Jesus' name, I dismantle the stronghold built on these things.

I stand on behalf of these individuals that they are fearfully, and wonderfully made. I declare this into the universe. Now angels pick up this prayer and minister healing and deliverance. I speak to every chain. Be broken and destroyed by the power of Jesus' mighty name. For this purpose was Jesus manifested, that he might destroy the works of the devil.

By the power of the Holy Spirit, the word of God, and the name of Jesus, I cancel distractions, forgetfulness, impulsive behavior, hyperactivity, fidgeting and restlessness.

In the name of Jesus, I apply the blood over these individuals by faith. I decree they are free by the blood of the lamb and the word of their testimony. In Jesus' name, I cast down anxiety, frustration, doubt, unbelief, fear, hopelessness, depression, and confusion.

Lord God, thank you for the promise to keep us in perfect peace when our minds are stayed on thee. Thank you Lord God that your word is spirit and it is life unto all those that find them and health to all their flesh, in Jesus' mighty name. Amen.

> *And Jesus went about all Galilee, teaching in their synagogues, preaching the gospel of the kingdom, and healing all kinds of sickness and all kinds of disease among the people."*
>
> *(Matthew 4:23)*

PRAYER REQUESTS JOURNAL

Use the following journal pages to write down
your prayer requests for healing or
the prayer requests of others.

Also use the space provided to record
your praise reports.

Prayer Requests

Prayer Requests

Prayer Requests

Prayer Requests

Praise Reports

Use the space below to record your healing and deliverance praise reports.

———— More Resources To Help ————

Be sure to order the companion CD for this book.
Digital downloads are also available for easy
listening on your computer or mobile devices.

With these powerful resources, you can read along
with Pastor Jamison as she prays,
declaring and decreeing your victory!

Order copies for your family and friends too.

Available at:
www.WatchmenPray.com

About the Author

Pastor Jamison is a powerful prayer warrior and intercessor. She walks in authority and power in the realm of the Spirit and has stood in the gap for many, bringing forth healing, deliverance and restoration. It is her passion to see God's people be built on a strong foundation of prayer and intercession, therefore she answered the call by establishing Watchmen on the Wall Prayer Network. Through the prayer network, she has torn down denominational barriers and connected prayer warriors and intercessors throughout the state of Florida and beyond.

Pastor Jamison serves as a spiritual midwife in the Kingdom of God, birthing many sons and daughters into their divine destinies through prayer, intercession and mentoring. This great Woman of God is also known as an anointed Bible teacher, bringing forth the Word with simplicity, clarity and power.

Read Pastor Jamison's testimony of deliverance at:
www.WatchmenPray.com

────────── Contact the Author ──────────

You are welcome to email or write the author with comments about this resource and her ministry. You are also welcome to contact her for bookings. As the Holy Spirit leads, Pastor Jamison is available for book club presentations, book signings, or speaking engagements for your church or organization (prayer group, women's ministries, women's clubs, conferences, workshops, retreats, and seminars).

Contact her at:
bettyjamison@bellsouth.net

Connect with her on social media:
https://www.facebook.com/betty.jamison.129

Mailing address:
P.O. Box 5866
Gainesville, Florida 32601

Need prayer support visit:
www.watchmenpray.com

www.ingramcontent.com/pod-product-compliance
Lightning Source LLC
Chambersburg PA
CBHW071222070526
44584CB00019B/3120